W9-CCB-040

Quivering Quakes

Teacher's Guide

Read Well 1 · Unit 31

Qu/qu

Qu says /qu/.
Quick Sound
Unvoiced

Critical Foundations in Primary Reading

Marilyn Sprick, Lisa Howard, Ann Fidanque, Shelley V. Jones

ISBN 13-digit: 978-1-59318-454-4   ISBN 10-digit: 1-59318-454-9   132038/2-10

9 10 11 12 RRDHRBVA 14 13 12 11

SOPRIS WEST EDUCATIONAL SERVICES
A CAMBIUM LEARNING COMPANY

BOSTON, MA • LONGMONT, CO

Table of Contents
Unit 31
Quivering Quakes

Important Tips

How to Teach the Lessons

I I Voiced (Word) **Unit A**	Mm /mmm/ **Monkey** Continuous Voiced **Unit B**	Ss /sss/ **Snake** Continuous Unvoiced **Unit 1**	Ee /eee/ **Emu** Continuous Voiced (Long) **Unit 2**	ee /eeee/ **Bee** Continuous Voiced (Long) **Unit 2**	Mm /mmm/ **Monkey** Continuous Voiced **Unit 3**
Aa /aaa/ **Ant** Continuous Voiced (Short) **Unit 4**	Dd /d/ **Dinosaur** Quick Voiced (not duh) **Unit 5**	th /ththth/ **the** Continuous Voiced **Unit 6**	Nn /nnn/ **Nest** Continuous Voiced **Unit 7**	Tt /t/ **Turkey** Quick Unvoiced (not tuh) **Unit 8**	Ww /www/ **Wind** Continuous Voiced (woo) **Unit 9**
Ii /iii/ **Insects** Continuous Voiced (Short) **Unit 10**	Th /Ththth/ **The** Continuous Voiced **Unit 10**	Hh /h/ **Hippo** Quick Unvoiced (not huh) **Unit 11**	Cc /c/ **Cat** Quick Unvoiced (not cuh) **Unit 12**	Rr /rrr/ **Rabbit** Continuous Voiced **Unit 13**	ea /eaeaea/ **Eagle** Continuous Voiced (Long) **Unit 13**
Sh/sh /shshsh/ **Sheep** Continuous Unvoiced **Unit 14**	Kk, -ck /k/ **Kangaroo** Quick Unvoiced (not kuh) **Unit 15**	oo /oooo/ **Moon** Continuous Voiced (Long) **Unit 16**	ar /ar/ **Shark** Voiced (R-Controlled) **Unit 17**	Wh/wh /wh/ **Whale** Quick Voiced **Unit 18**	Ee /ĕĕĕ/ **Engine or Ed** Continuous Voiced (Short) **Unit 19**
-y /-yyy/ **Fly** Continuous Voiced (Long) **Unit 20**	Ll /lll/ **Letter** Continuous Voiced **Unit 21**	Oo /ooo/ **Otter** Continuous Voiced (Short) **Unit 22**	Bb /b/ **Bat** Quick Voiced (not buh) **Unit 23**	all /all/ **Ball** Voiced **Unit 23**	Gg /g/ **Gorilla** Quick Voiced (not guh) **Unit 24**
Ff /fff/ **Frog** Continuous Unvoiced **Unit 25**	Uu /uuu/ **Umbrella** Continuous Voiced (Short) **Unit 26**	er /er/ **Sister** Voiced (R-Controlled) **Unit 27**	oo /oo/ **Book** Voiced (Short) **Unit 27**	Yy /y-/ **Yarn** Quick Voiced **Unit 28**	Aa /a/ **Ago** Voiced (Schwa) **Unit 28**
Pp /p/ **Pig** Quick Unvoiced (not puh) **Unit 29**	ay /ay/ **Hay** Voiced **Unit 29**	Vv /vvv/ **Volcano** Continuous Voiced **Unit 30**	Qu/qu /qu/ **Quake** Quick Unvoiced **Unit 31**	Jj /j/ **Jaguar** Quick Voiced (not juh) **Unit 32**	Xx /ksss/ **Fox** Continuous Unvoiced **Unit 33**
or /or/ **Horn** Voiced (R-Controlled) **Unit 33**	Zz /zzz/ **Zebra** Continuous Voiced **Unit 34**	a_e /a_e/ **Cake** Bossy E Voiced (Long) **Unit 34**	-y /-y/ **Baby** Voiced **Unit 35**	i_e /i_e/ **Kite** Bossy E Voiced (Long) **Unit 35**	ou /ou/ **Cloud** Voiced **Unit 36**
ow /ow/ **Cow** Voiced **Unit 36**	Ch/ch /ch/ **Chicken** Quick Unvoiced **Unit 37**	ai /ai/ **Rain** Voiced (Long) **Unit 37**	igh /igh/ **Flight** Voiced (Long) **Unit 38**	o_e /o_e/ **Bone** Bossy E Voiced (Long) **Unit 38**	ir /ir/ **Bird** Voiced (R-Controlled) **Unit 38**

Introduction
Quivering Quakes

Story Notes

What do you do when the earth is shaking? Drop, cover, and hold on. Unit 31 provides children with a smorgasbord of genres—nonfiction, realistic fiction, fiction with a legend, and a poem—all written around the theme of earthquakes.

Recommended Read Aloud

For reading outside of small group instruction

Earthquakes by Ellen J. Prager

Nonfiction • Expository

What are earthquakes and what causes them? A friendly crow reveals the answers while offering a bird's-eye view of earthquakes in action. Ellen Prager's clear, illuminating text is full of fun facts. Children learn that rocks inside the earth can break like an overstretched rubber band, causing the ground to shake and sway. Vibrant illustrations convey the sense of motion experienced in an earthquake.

Read Well Connection

Ellen Prager's read-aloud book is a perfect complement to the passages, stories, and poem provided in this unit. Children will enjoy comparing facts about earthquakes, what happens during an earthquake, and what they should do if there is one.

NOTE FROM THE AUTHORS

ENTHUSIASM

Your enthusiasm is contagious. Even though you may have read the *Read Well* stories with different groups, renew your interest each time you read the stories.

Young children's interest is a catalyst for repeated practice. Like a favorite bedtime story, children will not tire of reading the same story over and over if they are proud of their accomplishments and interested in the topic or story.

New and Important Objectives
A Research-Based Reading Program
Just Right for Young Children

Oral Language
Phonemic Awareness
Phonics
Fluency
Vocabulary
Comprehension

◆◆ Oral Language

In Units 21–38, language patterns are provided for high-frequency words and for some of the low-frequency words that are likely to require clarification. For English Language Learners and children with language delays, see page 10 for a list of the new high-frequency patterns.

Phonemic Awareness

Isolating Beginning, Middle, Ending Sounds, Segmenting, Blending, Rhyming, Onset and Rime

Qu says /qu/.
Quiver and quake,
/Qu/, /qu/, /qu/.

Quick Sound

Phonics

Letter Sounds and Combinations
☆ *Qu*
☆ *squ-*
Review • *Ss, Ee, ee, Mm, Aa, Dd, th, Nn, Tt, Ww, Ii, Th, Hh, Cc, Rr, ea, sh, Sh, Kk, -ck, oo, ar, wh, Wh, e* (short), *-y* (as in "fly"), *Ll, Oo, Bb, all, Gg, Ff, Uu, er, oo* (as in "book"), *Yy, a* (schwa), *Pp, ay, Vv*

Pattern Words
☆ *agree,* ☆ *always,* ☆ *apartment,* ☆ *bam,* ☆ *banquets,* ☆ *brick,* ☆ *bump,* ☆ *castle,* ☆ *clatter,* ☆ *click,* ☆ *clump,* ☆ *crashing,* ☆ *days,* ☆ *dresses,* ☆ *equipment,* ☆ *fear,* ☆ *finger,* ☆ *fingers,* ☆ *glass,* ☆ *hall,* ☆ *hearing,* ☆ *helping,* ☆ *Helps,* ☆ *hold,* ☆ *Hold,* ☆ *hop,* ☆ *hopping,* ☆ *hugs,* ☆ *kingdom,* ☆ *left,* ☆ *longer,* ☆ *lump,* ☆ *Nell,* ☆ *Nell's,* ☆ *old,* ☆ *quack,* ☆ *queen,* ☆ *Queen,* ☆ *quick,* ☆ *Quick,* ☆ *quilt,* ☆ *quintuplets,* ☆ *quit,* ☆ *Quit,* ☆ *quiver,* ☆ *reading,* ☆ *remembered,* ☆ *shatter,* ☆ *shook,* ☆ *silk,* ☆ *silver,* ☆ *singing,* ☆ *slipper,* ☆ *slippers,* ☆ *spent,* ☆ *squiggle,* ☆ *stronger,* ☆ *stump,* ☆ *sudden,* ☆ *thinker,* ☆ *thinkers,* ☆ *Thinkers,* ☆ *told,* ☆ *tumble,* ☆ *vet,* ☆ *visiting,* ☆ *walls,* ☆ *whatever,* ☆ *within,* ☆ *yelled,* ☆ *yelling*

Review • *across, after, After, ago, all, All, an, An, and, And, ask, asked, asleep, at, away, ball, back, bad, be, bed, beds, began, big, Big, but, called, can, call, clean, clock, cool, crash, cricket, crust, Crust, day, Day, deep, did, Did, drop, Drop, ever, fall, fast, feel, fell, get, glad, got, grinned, grumble, had, happen, happens, hard, hear, help, Help, her, Her, hid, hundred, if, If, I'm, in, it, It, It's, kid, land, layer, Layer, layers, let, little, long, look, Mack, mad, may, me, mess, met, mom, Mom, must, my, My, need, never, No,*

◆◆ = Oral language patterns   ☆ = New in this unit

Pattern Words *(continued)*

nodded, not, off, on, pet, pick, plan, red, remember, Remember, resting, ring, rings, rumble, sad, sang, say, seem, she, She, small, so, soon, Soon, stand, stick, still, stop, strong, Sweet, tall, team, tell, Tell, thank, Thank, that, them, Then, things, Things, this, This, three, Three, too, top, Top, trick, under, understand, until, up, us, wall, we, We, well, went, wet, Wham, when, When, why, Why, will, wink, wish, with, year

Tricky Words

★*build,* ★*buildings,* ★*cover,* ★*Cover,* ★*earthquake,* ★*Earthquake,* ★*earthquakes,* ★*Earthquakes,* ★*earthquake's,* ★*listened,* ★*people's,* ★*please,* ★*Please,* ★*servants,* ★*very,* ★*worker*

Review • *a, A, about, America, animals, are, Are, as, brother, could, do, earth, earth's, even, friend, friends, from, great, has, have, I, is, Is, isn't, listen, Listen, live, of, Of, often, one, One, people, said, should, Should, the, The, there, they, They, to, together, two, want, wanted, was, were, what, What, What's, where, words, work, worked, would, you, your*

Comprehension

Comprehension Strategies

Priming Background Knowledge, Building Knowledge, Making Connections, Predicting, Identifying, Describing, Demonstrating, Defining, Explaining, Inferring, Summarizing, Locating Information, Monitoring Comprehension, Sequencing

Story Elements

Title, Where (Setting), Who (Character), Problem, What (Action)

Story Vocabulary

★Servant, ★Queen

Text Structure

Beginning, Middle, End

Expository Elements

Facts

Genre

Nonfiction • Expository

Fiction • Realistic Narrative

Fiction • Legend

Poem

Lessons

Legends were used by people long ago to explain why natural events occurred.

★Earthquakes can be understood through science.

Written Response

Sentence Illustration, Sentence Completion, Sentence Writing, Sentence Comprehension—Multiple Choice, Summarizing—Story Map, Conventions—Beginning Capital, Period

Fluency

Accuracy, Expression, Phrasing, Rate

Daily Lesson Planning

PACING

Some students will begin the process of learning to read slowly but make rapid progress later. If students complete Unit 38 by the end of the year, they will be at or above a beginning second grade reading level. Groups that are working at a slower pace may require more intensive *Read Well* instruction and practice. (See *Getting Started: A Guide to Implementation.*)

ASSESSMENT

Upon completion of this unit, assess each student and proceed to Unit 32 as appropriate.

SAMPLE LESSON PLANS

The sample lesson plans illustrate how materials can be used for students with different learning needs. Each lesson plan is designed to provide daily decoding practice and story reading.

WEAK PASS CAUTION

If a student or students receive a Weak Pass on the previous two units, do not simply continue forward. See "Making Decisions" for Intervention Options.

Note: The 2-Day Plan is no longer suggested. Depending on time variables, high-performing students may be able to read stories 2, 4, and 6 independently.

3-DAY PLAN		
Day 1	**Day 2**	**Day 3**
• Decoding Practice 1	• Decoding Practice 2	• Decoding Practice 3
• Stories 1 and 2	• Stories 3 and 4	• Stories 5 and 6
• Comprehension Work 1b*	• Comprehension Work 3*	• Comprehension Work 5*
• Comprehension Work 2*	• Comprehension Work 4*	• Skill Work 6* (Optional)
• Homework 1, Story 2*	• Homework 2, Story 4*	• Homework 3, Story 6*
		• Homework 4, Storybook Decoding Review*

To avoid excessive seatwork, 3- and 4-Day Plans omit or adjust use of Skill Work. If appropriate, Skill Work 1a and 6b can be used anytime during or after this unit as independent work or homework.

4-DAY PLAN			
Day 1	**Day 2**	**Day 3**	**Day 4**
• Decoding Practice 1	• Decoding Practice 2	• Decoding Practice 3	• Decoding Practice 4
• Stories 1 and 2	• Stories 3 and 4	• Stories 5 and 6	• Review Stories 2, 4, and 6
• Comprehension Work 1b*	• Comprehension Work 3*	• Comprehension Work 5*	• Skill Work 6*
• Comprehension Work 2*	• Comprehension Work 4*	• Homework 3, Story 6*	• Homework 4, Storybook Decoding Review*
• Homework 1, Story 2*	• Homework 2, Story 4*		

---

* From *Read Well* Comprehension and Skill Work (workbook), *Read Well* Homework (blackline masters), or Extra Practice in this book.

6-DAY PLAN • *Pre-Intervention*

Day 1	Day 2	Day 3
• Decoding Practice 1 • Story 1 • Skill Work 1a* (Optional) • Comprehension Work 1b*	• Review Decoding Practice 1 • Story 2 • Comprehension Work 2* • Homework 1, Story 2*	• Decoding Practice 2 • Story 3 • Comprehension Work 3*
Day 4	**Day 5**	**Day 6**
• Review Decoding Practice 2 • Story 4 • Comprehension Work 4* • Homework 2, Story 4*	• Decoding Practice 3 • Story 5 • Comprehension Work 5* • Homework 4, Storybook Decoding Review*	• Decoding Practice 4 • Story 6 • Skill Work 6* • Homework 3, Story 6*

PRE-INTERVENTION AND INTERVENTION

See *Getting Started: A Guide to Implementation* for information on how to achieve mastery at a faster pace with students who require six or more days of instruction.

8-DAY PLAN • *Intervention*

Day 1	Day 2	Day 3	Day 4
• Decoding Practice 1 • Story 1 • Skill Work 1a* (Optional) • Comprehension Work 1b*	• Review Decoding Practice 1 • Story 2 • Comprehension Work 2* • Homework 1, Story 2*	• Decoding Practice 2 • Story 3 • Comprehension Work 3*	• Review Decoding Practice 2 • Story 4 • Comprehension Work 4* • Homework 2, Story 4*
Day 5	**Day 6**	**Day 7**	**Day 8**
• Decoding Practice 3 • Story 5 • Comprehension Work 5* • Homework 4, Storybook Decoding Review*	• Decoding Practice 4 • Story 6 • Skill Work 6* • Homework 3, Story 6*	• Extra Practice 1* • Extra Practice 1 Fluency Passage*	• Extra Practice 2* • Extra Practice 2 Fluency Passages*

10-DAY PLAN • *Intervention*

Day 1	Day 2	Day 3	Day 4	Day 5
• Decoding Practice 1 • Story 1 • Skill Work 1a* (Optional) • Comprehension Work 1b*	• Review Decoding Practice 1 • Story 2 • Comprehension Work 2* • Homework 1, Story 2*	• Decoding Practice 2 • Story 3 • Comprehension Work 3*	• Review Decoding Practice 2 • Story 4 • Comprehension Work 4* • Homework 2, Story 4*	• Decoding Practice 3 • Story 5 • Comprehension Work 5* • Homework 4, Storybook Decoding Review*
Day 6	**Day 7**	**Day 8**	**Day 9**	**Day 10**
• Decoding Practice 4 • Story 6 • Skill Work 6* • Homework 3, Story 6*	• Extra Practice 1* • Extra Practice 1 Fluency Passage*	• Extra Practice 2* • Extra Practice 2 Fluency Passages*	• Extra Practice 3* • Extra Practice 3 Fluency Passage*	• Extra Practice 4* • Extra Practice 4 Fluency Passage*

Materials and Materials Preparation

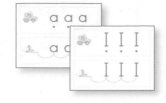

Core Lessons

Teacher Materials

READ WELL MATERIALS

- Unit 31 Teacher's Guide
- Sound and Word Cards for Units 1–31
- Game markers (optional for use with cover-up activities)
- *Assessment Manual* or page 54

SCHOOL SUPPLIES

- Stopwatch or watch with a second hand

Student Materials

READ WELL MATERIALS

- Decoding Book 4 for each student
- Unit 31 Storybook for each student
- Unit 31 Comprehension and Skill Work for each student (My Activity Book 4)
- Unit 31 Certificate of Achievement (blackline master page 55)
- Unit 31 Homework for each student (blackline masters)
  See *Getting Started* for suggested homework routines.

SCHOOL SUPPLIES

- Pencils, colors (optional—markers, crayons, or colored pencils)

> Make one copy per student of each blackline master as appropriate for the group.
>
> *Note:* For new or difficult Comprehension and Skill Work activities, make overhead transparencies from the blackline masters. Use the transparencies to demonstrate and guide practice.

Extra Practice Lessons

Note: Use these lessons only if needed.

Student Materials

READ WELL MATERIALS

- Unit 31 Extra Practice 1 and 2 for each student (blackline master pages 57 and 61)
- Unit 31 Extra Practice 1, 2, 3, and 4 Fluency Passages for each student (blackline master pages 58, 62, 64, 66)
- Take-Home Game (blackline master page 59)

SCHOOL SUPPLIES

- Pencils, colors (markers, crayons, or colored pencils)
- White boards or paper

Important Tips

In this section, you will find:

☆ More About Monitoring Comprehension and Locating Information

Some children naturally monitor their own comprehension—knowing what they know and what they do not know. Other children can benefit from demonstration and guided practice. Read the sample scripted lesson for another example of procedures.

Pacing

Review where your students are and project where they will be at the end of the year using the worksheet on page 9.

Language and Vocabulary Practice— Review and High-Frequency Words

An additional focus on vocabulary and language skills often benefits English Language Learners and students with language delays.

Periodically, review important words to build a base of knowledge.

A list of oral language patterns used with high-frequency words is also provided for additional emphasis and practice across settings.

★More About Monitoring Comprehension and Locating Information

PURPOSE

If students would benefit, continue to explicitly teach students how to monitor their own comprehension and to locate information. Have students review how to follow the direction "If you need to, look in your book."

PROCEDURES

Demonstrate, guide practice, and then provide independent practice with support as needed. For each Comprehension Work Activity, repeat this process until students are able to work independently.

Example

Everyone, look at the top of your page.
Read the direction. What does it say?
If you need to, look in your book.

Read the title of your Comprehension Work.
It says ... Facts About an "E-blank."
What goes in the blank? (Earthquake)
I don't think I know how to spell "Earthquake,"
so what should I do? (Look in your book.)

Point in your book. That's right. Here is the word "Earthquake."

Read the first part of item 1. (The earth has "blank" layers.) Do you remember the answer? (Three)
That's what I remember. Nod your head if you're sure of the answer. Do we need to look in our books? (No)

Read the next part of item 1. (The top layer is called the "blank.") I think the word that goes in the blank is "earth," but I'm not sure. [Katrina], what do you think it should say?
(I think it should say "The top layer is called the crust.")
Since we aren't sure, what should we do? (Look in our books.)

That's right. Raise your hand when you find where it tells us what the top layer of the earth is called ...

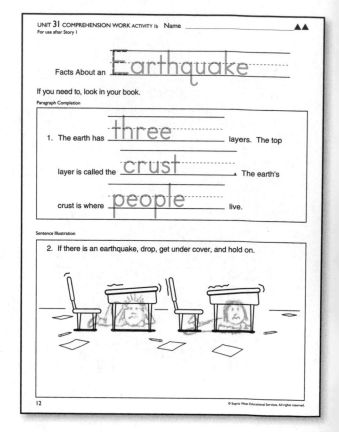

Use the information in the book to affirm student responses. Repeat with the remaining items as needed and with subsequent Comprehension Work activities.

Pacing

RATE OF LEARNING

Learning curves vary throughout the school year. Make adjustments in the number of days per unit based on student needs. Mastery learning takes precedence over getting through the program.

GRADE LEVEL

First grade children who complete *Read Well 1*, Unit 38, with mastery prior to the end of the school year should proceed to *Read Well Plus*. These children will be performing above grade level. Individual students or groups that may not complete *Read Well 1*, Unit 38, by the end of first grade may benefit from more intensive practice, summer school, and/or completion in second grade.

INTENSIVE *READ WELL* INSTRUCTION

Intensive *Read Well* instruction can be accomplished by dedicating 90 minutes to each small group, five days per week, and/or double dosing students in *Read Well*. (See *Getting Started: A Guide to Implementation*.)

END-OF-YEAR PROJECTION

To determine where students will be at the end of the year at the current pace of instruction:

1. Identify the current unit _____

2. Identify the number of days per unit _____

3. Identify the number of days remaining in the school year _____

4. Identify the number of units projected for completion _____

    Divide the number of days remaining in the school year by the number of days per unit.

    _____ number of days remaining in school year ÷ _____ number of days per unit

    = _____ additional number of units projected for completion

5. Identify the last unit to be completed at the current rate of instruction _____

    Add the current unit number with the number of units projected for completion.

    _____ current unit number + _____ additional number of units projected = _____ ending unit

Language and Vocabulary Practice Review and High-Frequency Words

PURPOSE

The following lessons may be used to augment a structured oral language program. Periodic review is important to maintain knowledge and use of vocabulary words.

◆◆ **FOR ENGLISH LANGUAGE LEARNERS AND CHILDREN WITH LANGUAGE DELAYS**

REVIEW "RELATIVES"

Collect and review pictures of relatives. Have students draw a picture of their relatives.

- Help students review the word "relatives."

  You know the special word for people in your family.
  The word is . . . relatives.

- Have students identify relatives in a picture. Say something like:

  Look at the picture. Let's see if we can figure out who is in the picture.
  It shows a mother, a father, two . . . sisters, and a grandfather.
  They are part of the family so they are . . . relatives.

- Have students draw a picture of their relatives. Say something like:

  Draw a picture of your family. You can include your mother, father, brothers, sisters, grandparents, and uncles and aunts.

- Have students talk about their pictures.

  [Ahmed], who is in your picture?
  Everyone, the people in [Ahmed's] picture are his . . . relatives.

REVIEW "LEGEND."

- Collect simple legends from different cultures, particularly from the ethnic backgrounds of the children in your classroom.
- Review the word "legend" and give examples of its meaning. Say something like:

  You learned the word "legend." Tell me the word. (Legend)
  What kind of story did people tell to explain things they saw? (Legends)
  A story that explains why we have floods is called a . . . (legend).
  A story that explains why we have thunderstorms is called a . . . (legend).

ORAL LANGUAGE PATTERNS USED WITH NEW HIGH-FREQUENCY WORDS

In addition to the selected vocabulary word for each selection, *Read Well* Decoding Practices include simple sentences for all new high-frequency words. The sentences are repeated below for additional language practice.

ORAL LANGUAGE PATTERNS
★ High-Frequency Words Introduced in This Unit
★ always – We *always* go to recess after lunch. What do we *always* do?
★ hold – Show me how to *hold* [onto the table]. Show me how to *hold* [your book].
★ never – You should *never* [play with matches]. When should you [play with matches]? *(Never)*
★ old – If you live to be 100, you will be . . . *old.*
★ please – If you want something, say . . . *(please).*
★ very – I am not just a little [happy], I am . . . *very* [happy].

How to Teach the Lessons

Teach from this section. Each instructional component is outlined in an easy-to-teach format. Special tips are provided to help you nurture student progress.

Decoding Practice 1

- Unit Introduction
- Story 1, Duet
- Skill Work Activity 1a
- Comprehension Work Activity 1b
- Story 2, Solo
- Comprehension Work Activity 2

Decoding Practice 2

- Story 3, Duet
- Comprehension Work Activity 3
- Story 4, Solo
- Comprehension Work Activity 4

Decoding Practice 3

- Story 5, Duet
- Comprehension Work Activity 5
- Story 6, Solo
- Skill Work Activity 6

Decoding Practice 4

Review Solo Stories

BUILDING INDEPENDENCE
Next Steps • Principles of Instruction

For Units 21–38, follow the scaffolded principles of instruction below.

Provide demonstration and/or guided practice only with:
- New sounds
- Pattern words with new sounds
- New Tricky Words
- New multisyllabic words

Provide independent practice (practice without your assistance or voice) on:
- New and review pattern words with known sounds
- Review Tricky Words
- Review multisyllabic words

If students make errors, provide appropriate corrections.
- Have students identify any difficult sound and then sound out the word. Provide discrimination practice.
- Reintroduce difficult Tricky Words based on the initial introduction procedures.

If students require your assistance on words with known sounds, evaluate placement and consider a Jell-Well Review.

1 SOUND REVIEW

2 NEW SOUND INTRODUCTION

3 NEW SOUND PRACTICE

4 SOUNDING OUT SMOOTHLY

- For each word, have students say the underlined part, sound out the word, and then read the word.
  Use the words in sentences as needed.
- Provide repeated practice. Mix group and individual turns, independent of your voice.

◆◆ 5 MORE SOUNDING OUT SMOOTHLY

- Have students sound out each word, and then read the word.
  Use the words in sentences as needed.
- Provide repeated practice. Mix group and individual turns, independent of your voice.

6 MULTISYLLABIC WORDS

- In the Pencil Row, have students read the word part "earth." Tell them the next part, "quake," then have students read the whole word. Say something like:
  Read the first part. (earth)
  The next part is "quake." Read the next part. (quake)
  Now read the whole word. (earthquake)
- For the word "apartment," tell students that they are going to read a very big word. Explain that they can read this word by reading each part and then the whole word.
- Repeat with the Flower Row.
- Provide repeated practice. Mix group and individual turns, independent of your voice.

◆◆ 7 ACCURACY AND FLUENCY BUILDING
★ **New Tricky Word: "very"**
Tell students the new Tricky Word "very" and then have them read it several times.
Repeat practice on each column, building accuracy first and then fluency.

8 DAILY STORY READING
Proceed to the Unit 31 Storybook. See Daily Lesson Planning for pacing suggestions.

9 COMPREHENSION AND SKILL WORK ACTIVITY I AND/OR ACTIVITY 2
See pages 20, 21, and/or 25.

Note: The light scripting in *Read Well* will help you visualize instruction as you prepare for a lesson. Scripting provides an instructional guide and is not intended to be memorized or read to students.

UNIT 31 DECODING PRACTICE I
(For use with Stories 1 and 2)

1. SOUND REVIEW Use Sound Cards for Units 1–30.

2. NEW SOUND INTRODUCTION Have students echo (repeat) the phrases. Do not have students read the poem.

<u>Qu</u> as in Quake

The letter <u>q</u> goes with <u>u</u>.

<u>Qu</u> says qu.

Quiver and quake,

Qu, qu, qu.

3. NEW SOUND PRACTICE Have students read, trace, and say /qu/.

Qu   qu

4. SOUNDING OUT SMOOTHLY For each word, have students say the underlined part, then sound out the word and read it.

☆ <u>Qu</u>een   <u>qu</u>ick   <u>qu</u>it

5. MORE SOUNDING OUT SMOOTHLY Have students sound out each word in one smooth breath, then read the word.

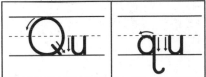

| ■ | deep | bump | hop | hugs |
| ▲ | live | layers | never | crust | glass |

6. MULTISYLLABIC WORDS Have students say each word part, then read the whole word.

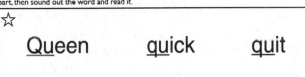

| ✏ | earth•quake = earthquake | a•part•ment = apartment |
| ✿ | a•sleep = asleep | re•mem•ber = remember |

★7. ACCURACY/FLUENCY BUILDING Have students read each word in the column. Next, have students practice the column.

♥	●	✈ Tricky Words
clatter	crashing	★very
shatter	hopping	even
sudden	yelling	earth
happen	hearing	of

8. DAILY STORY READING

5

Sentence Suggestions: If a sentence is included, use it *after* decoding the individual word. The sentences may be used to build oral language patterns and vocabulary. Use of sentences also emphasizes that words have meaning.

❶ INTRODUCING THE UNIT AND THE TITLE PAGE

Identifying—Title

Tell students this unit is about earthquakes. The story is "Quivering Quakes."

Remind students that the whole book is called *Earth Science*.

Priming Background Knowledge

Ask students what they already know about earthquakes.

Explain to students that the unit has a factual passage about earthquakes, two made-up stories, and a poem.

❷ INTRODUCING VOCABULARY

Vocabulary—Servant, Queen

Servant

Put your finger under the first picture.

A *servant* is a person who has a job waiting on others.

Servants are people who might cook and clean for others.

Queen

Put your finger under the next picture.

A *queen* is a woman who is the leader of her country or kingdom.

Quivering Quakes

Illustrated by Allan Eitzen

An Earthquake
By Marilyn Sprick

The Legend of Queen Nell
By Marilyn Sprick and Jessica Sprick

Drop, Cover, and Hold
By Shelley V. Jones

UNIT 31 STORIES

Vocabulary Words

servant
A servant is a person who has a job waiting on others.

queen
A queen is a woman who is a leader of her country or kingdom.

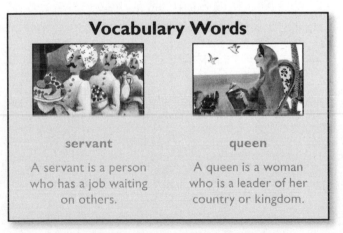

Vocabulary Words

servant
A servant is a person who has a job waiting on others.

queen
A queen is a woman who is a leader of her country or kingdom.

Defining Vocabulary—Servant, Queen

DUET STORY READING INSTRUCTIONS

Students read from their own storybooks.
The teacher reads the small text and students read the large text.

PACING

- 3- to 4-Day Plans: Have students do the first reading of Duet Story 1.
  Then proceed to repeated readings of Solo Story 2.
- 6- to 10-Day Plans: Have students do the first *and* second readings.

COMPREHENSION BUILDING:
DISCUSSION QUESTIONS AND TEACHER THINK ALOUDS

- Ask questions and discuss text on the first reading when indicated in the storybook in light gray text.
- Encourage students to answer questions with complete sentences when appropriate. Following a response, acknowledge the accuracy of the response.
- If students have difficulty with a comprehension question, think aloud with them or reread the portion of the story that answers the question. Then, ask the question again.

PROCEDURES

1. First Reading

Mix group and individual turns on student-read sentences. On individual turns, gently correct any error, and then have the student reread the text.

2. Second Reading

Repeat the reading only as needed for comprehension.

An Earthquake

CHAPTER 1

What Is an Earthquake?

What causes an earthquake?[1]

This is the earth. Remember, the earth has three layers. The top layer of the earth is called the crust. The earth's crust is very deep.

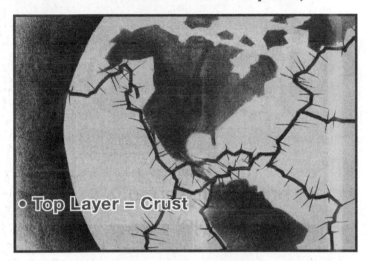

Top Layer = Crust

See the picture. Deep under the earth's surface, the crust is made up of big pieces of hard rock called plates. The plates are outlined in red.

Trace the plates with your fingers.[2]

When the plates move, they sometimes bump and scrape against each other. The land vibrates and shakes as the plates bump and scrape.

When this happens, we feel an earthquake.

What happens when the plates bump and scrape against each other?[3]

24

❶ **Building Knowledge**

❷ **Demonstrating—Where**

❸ **Explaining** (The land vibrates and shakes.)

Note: Questions focus students on important story elements and provide prompts for story discussions. Answers provide guidance, not verbatim responses.

What happens in an earthquake?

Earthquakes can be big and they can be small. A small earthquake is quick. If an earthquake is small, you may ask, "What was that bump? Did you feel that?"

Though a small earthquake may feel like a quick little jiggle, a big earthquake can be very violent and scary. Luckily, big earthquakes don't happen very often.

What is happening in the picture?**I** How do you think the boy and girl feel?**2**

25

❶ **Describing** (Things are falling from the shelves . . .)

❷ **Inferring**

What should you do in a big earthquake?

In a big earthquake, you may hear a rumble. The ground will vibrate and shake. If you are in a big earthquake, it is important to drop, get under cover, and hold on.

What should you do during an earthquake? **1**

When an earthquake happens, it may seem as if it will never stop, but even a big earthquake is quick. Big earthquakes do not happen often. If you feel an earthquake, remember what to do. Then, remember that the earthquake will stop soon.

26

❶ Identifying—Action (You should drop, get under cover, and hold on.)

SOUND PAGE

Use work pages from the workbook.

CHECKOUT OPPORTUNITY

While students are working on Comprehension and Skill Work, you may wish to listen to individuals read a Decoding Practice or Solo Story. If the student makes an error, gently correct and have the student reread the column, row, or sentence.

PROCEDURES

For each step, demonstrate and guide practice as needed.

1. Handwriting—Basic Instructions

- Have students identify the capital letter combination Qu.
- Have students trace and write the capital letter combination Qu— leaving a finger space between each combination. Repeat with the small letter combination qu on the next rows.
- In each row have students circle their best letter combination.

2. Coloring—Basic Instructions

Have students color the picture, using at least three colors.

Note: Neat work helps students take pride in their efforts. Periodically, comment on students' progress and best efforts.

FACT REVIEW

Use work pages from the workbook.

Monitoring Comprehension
Locating Information →

Writing, Identifying—Facts →

Illustrating—Action →

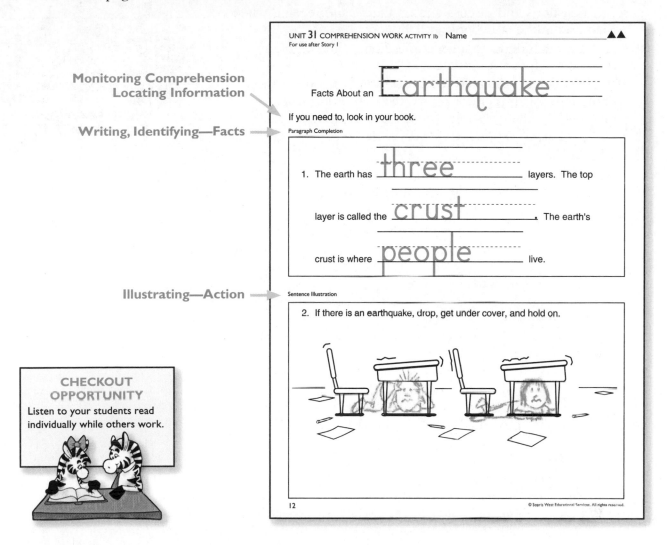

CHECKOUT OPPORTUNITY
Listen to your students read individually while others work.

PROCEDURES

For each step, demonstrate and guide practice as needed.

- (Demonstrate) Have students orally respond to items while you demonstrate how to complete the page.
- (Guide) Have students orally respond to the items, but do not demonstrate how to complete the page.
- (Independent With Support) Have students silently read over the items and ask any questions they may have.

1. Paragraph Completion—Basic Instructions (Item 1)

Have students read and complete the sentences.

2. Sentence Illustration—Specific Instructions (Item 2)

- Have students read the sentence about what to do in an earthquake.
- Then, have them draw a picture of what to do in an earthquake.

Note: Periodically, demonstrate how to complete a Sentence Illustration. You may wish to show students how to add details to the picture and/or color neatly to the edges.

SOLO STORY READING INSTRUCTIONS

Students read from their own storybooks.

- Ask questions and discuss text on the *second* reading when indicated in the storybook in light gray text.
- Encourage students to answer questions with complete sentences when appropriate.
- If students have difficulty with a comprehension question, think aloud with them or reread the portion of the story that answers the question. Then, ask the question again.

PROCEDURES

1. First Reading

- Have students individually whisper read the story, using their fingers to track text.
- After students complete the first reading and before the second reading, have students practice a few paragraphs. First demonstrate expressive reading for students, then give individual turns. Acknowledge student efforts.

2. Second Reading

- Mix group and individual turns, independent of your voice. Have students work toward an accuracy goal of 0–2 errors. Quietly keep track of errors made by all students in each group.
- After reading the story, practice any difficult words.
- If the group has not reached the accuracy goal, have the group reread the story, mixing group and individual turns.

3. Repeated Readings
a. Timed Readings

- Once the accuracy goal has been achieved, have individual students read the page while the other children track the text with their fingers and whisper read.

  Time individuals for 30 seconds and encourage each student to work for a personal best.

- Count the number of words read correctly in 30 seconds (words read minus errors). Multiply by two to determine words correct per minute. Record student scores.

Note: If a student is unable to read with close to 100% accuracy, the personal goal should be accuracy. If the student is unable to read with accuracy, evaluate group placement and consider a Jell-Well Review.

b. Partner Reading

During students' daily independent work, have them do Partner Reading.

c. Homework 1

Have students read the story at home. (A reprint of this story is available on a blackline master in *Read Well* Homework.)

CHAPTER 2

The Day of the Earthquake

What is this story about? **1**

One day, we had a big earthquake where I live. My brother, Mack, and I were asleep when all of a sudden the beds began to hop.

FINGER TRACKING (Reminder)
Continue having children track the large text with their fingers.

My brother asked, "What's that?" Then my clock fell off the wall. Quick as a wink, we were under the beds.

My, what a clatter! We could hear glass shatter. "Wham, bam, crash!"

We hid until the beds quit hopping. We hid until things quit crashing. Soon all was still.

What did the boys do? **2** Were they safe? **3** How do you think they felt? **4**

27

❶ **Identifying—What** (The story is about an earthquake.)

❷ **Identifying—Action** (The boys hid under the beds.)

❸ **Inferring**

❹ **Inferring**

STORY 2, SOLO

Then I remember hearing my mom. She was yelling, "It's me. I'm cool. Are you cool?" We all got big hugs.

After the earthquake, the apartment was one big mess. Mom said, "My, my, my." Then she grinned, and we grinned back.

After the earthquake, the apartment was a mess. Why did the boys' mother grin?**1** Why did the boys grin?**2**

28

❶ **Inferring** (The boy's mother was glad that everyone was okay.)

❷ **Inferring** (The boys grinned because they were glad the earthquake was over.)

STORY COMPREHENSION
Use work pages from the workbook.

Monitoring Comprehension
Locating Information

Writing
Identifying—Who
Conventions—Period

Writing
Complete Sentence
Explaining
Conventions—Beginning Capital,
Period

Writing
Identifying—What
Conventions—Period

Writing
Identifying—Action
Conventions—Period

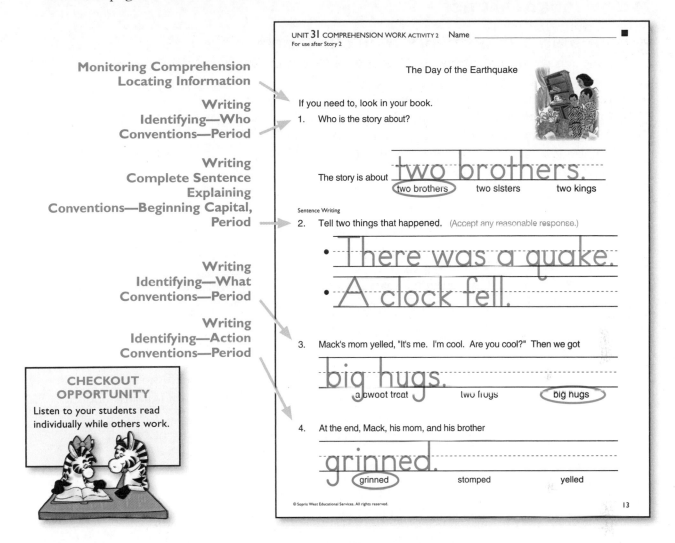

UNIT **31** COMPREHENSION WORK ACTIVITY 2   Name _____   ■
For use after Story 2

The Day of the Earthquake

If you need to, look in your book.
1. Who is the story about?

The story is about ̲t̲w̲o̲ ̲b̲r̲o̲t̲h̲e̲r̲s̲.̲
(two brothers)   two sisters   two kings

Sentence Writing
2. Tell two things that happened. (Accept any reasonable response.)

• There was a quake.
• A clock fell.

3. Mack's mom yelled, "It's me. I'm cool. Are you cool?" Then we got
̲b̲i̲g̲ ̲h̲u̲g̲s̲.̲
a sweet treat   two frogs   (big hugs)

4. At the end, Mack, his mom, and his brother
̲g̲r̲i̲n̲n̲e̲d̲.̲
(grinned)   stomped   yelled

© Sopris West Educational Services. All rights reserved.   13

CHECKOUT OPPORTUNITY
Listen to your students read individually while others work.

PROCEDURES
For each step, demonstrate and guide practice as needed.

1. Multiple Choice, Sentence Completion—Basic Instructions
(Items 1, 3, 4)
- Have students select and circle the word or words that correctly complete the sentences. Periodically, think aloud with students. Discuss the multiple choice options. As appropriate, ask questions like: "Does the first answer make sense?" "Is that what the book said?" "Is the answer completely correct?"
- Have them write answers in the blanks and place a period at the end as appropriate.

2. Sentence Writing—Basic Instructions (Item 2)
- Have students read the direction and brainstorm possible responses, using complete sentences.
- Have students write complete sentences that start with a capital and end with a period.

① SOUND REVIEW

② NEW SOUND PRACTICE

③ SOUNDING OUT SMOOTHLY, MAIN CHARACTER
- For each word, have students say the underlined part, then sound out the word, and read it.
- Repeat practice until students can read the two words fluently.
- Introduce the Unit 31 main character, Queen Nell. Say something like:

  Our new story happened long ago, in a faraway land.

  It is about a beautiful young queen named Queen Nell.

  Who is the main character? (Queen Nell)

④ SOUNDING OUT SMOOTHLY

Provide repeated practice. Mix group and individual turns, independent of your voice.

◆◆ **⑤ MULTISYLLABIC WORDS**
- In the Circle Row, have students read the word part "king." Tell them the word part "dom" and them have them read the whole word. Say something like:

  Read the first part. (king)

  The next part is tricky. Say /dum/. (dom)

  Now read the whole word. (kingdom)

  For the word "hundred," have students say each word part, then read the whole word.
- In the Heart Row, tell students that the first word part in "always" sounds just like the word "all."
- Provide repeated practice. Mix group and individual turns, independent of your voice.

⑥ ACCURACY AND FLUENCY BUILDING

Repeat practice on each column, building accuracy first and then fluency.

◆◆ **⑦ TRICKY WORDS**

★ **New Tricky Words: "please" and "servants"**
- Have students look at the first Tricky Word, "please."

  Tell them the second e is crossed out because it is silent—it doesn't say anything.

  Have students sound out "please," read it five times, and use it in oral sentences.
- Have students look at the next Tricky Word, "servants." Say something like:

  Let's try sounding out the Tricky Word. /ssservvvaaannntsss/

  Here's how you say the word "servants."

  Some workers are called servants.

  Have students read "servants" five times and use it in oral sentences.
- Have students read the row. Repeat, mixing group and individual turns, independent of your voice. Use the words in sentences as needed.

⑧ DAILY STORY READING

Proceed to the Unit 31 Storybook. See Daily Lesson Planning for pacing suggestions.

⑨ COMPREHENSION AND SKILL WORK ACTIVITY 3 AND/OR ACTIVITY 4

See pages 32, 33, and/or 37.

◆◆ For ELLs and children with language delays, provide repeated and extended practice with the language patterns. See page 10 for tips.

UNIT **31** DECODING PRACTICE 2
(For use with Stories 3 and 4)

1. SOUND REVIEW Use Sound Cards for Units 1–31 or Sound Review on Decoding Practice 4.

2. NEW SOUND PRACTICE Have students read, trace, and say /qu/.

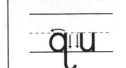 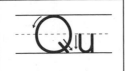

3. SOUNDING OUT SMOOTHLY, MAIN CHARACTER
For each word, have students sound out the word and read it. Introduce the Unit 31 main character, Queen Nell.

Queen Nell

4. SOUNDING OUT SMOOTHLY For each word, have students say the underlined part, sound out the word in one smooth breath, and then read the word.

■ <u>qu</u>iver   g<u>l</u>ass   sp<u>e</u>nt   <u>si</u>lk   d<u>re</u>sses

5. MULTISYLLABIC WORDS Have students say each word part, then read the whole word.

● king•dom = kingdom   hun•dred = hundred

♥ vis•it•ing = visiting   al•ways = always

6. ACCURACY/FLUENCY BUILDING For each column, have students read each word, then practice the column.

✈	✏	✿
worked	tumble	stronger
worker	grumble	silver
build	look	slipper
buildings	shook	finger

BUILDING INDEPENDENCE
(Reminder)
Provide demonstration and guided practice only as needed.

◆◆ **SENTENCE SUGGESTIONS**

■ quiver – When you *quiver*, you shake. Show me a *quiver*.

● kingdom – A *kingdom* is a country with a king or queen.

♥ always – We *always* go to recess after lunch. What do we *always* do?

▲ please – If you want something, say . . . (*please*).

★7. TRICKY WORDS See Teacher's Guide for how to introduce "please" and "servants." Next, have students silently figure out each word and read it aloud.

▲   ★pleas<s>e</s>   ★<u>servants</u>   people   your

8. DAILY STORY READING

6

Sentence Suggestions: Use the appropriate suggested sentence *after* decoding each individual word.

DUET STORY READING INSTRUCTIONS

Students read from their own storybooks.

The teacher reads the small text and students read the large text.

PACING

- 3- to 4-Day Plans: Have students do the first reading of Duet Story 3.

  Then proceed to repeated readings of Solo Story 4.
- 6- to 10-Day Plans: Have students do the first *and* second readings.

COMPREHENSION BUILDING:
DISCUSSION QUESTIONS AND TEACHER THINK ALOUDS

- Ask questions and discuss text on the first reading when indicated in the storybook in light gray text.
- Encourage students to answer questions with complete sentences when appropriate.
- If students have difficulty with a comprehension question, think aloud with them or reread the portion of the story that answers the question. Then, ask the question again.

PROCEDURES

1. First Reading

Mix group and individual turns on student-read sentences. On individual turns, gently correct any error, and then have the student reread the text.

2. Second Reading

Repeat the reading only as needed for comprehension.

The Legend of Queen Nell

CHAPTER I

Sweet Queen Nell

Long, long ago, in a faraway land, there was a beautiful young queen. From the time she was born, Queen Nell had been given whatever she wanted.

Queen Nell had one hundred servants. Her servants got Nell whatever she wanted, but Nell always remembered to say "please" and "thank you."

FOCUS ON VOCABULARY

After reading the title of the story, say something like: This story is also a legend. A legend is a story that . . . explains why something happens. What do you think this legend will explain?

29

Queen Nell loved beautiful things.

Queen Nell had long, red, silk dresses. She had slippers of glass and silver rings on her fingers.

Queen Nell spent her days resting, visiting with friends, reading, and singing. All was fine for Queen Nell. She had a good life in her beautiful palace by the sea.

Tell me what Queen Nell's life was like.

❶ **Describing** (Queen Nell spent her days resting, visiting friends, reading, and singing. She had a good life.)

Then, one day there was a deep grumble from within the earth. The earth began to quiver. Then the earth shook. Things began to tumble from the walls. Queen Nell hid under her big, strong bed. My, what a clatter! She could hear things shatter. "Wham, bam, crash!"

What do you think was happening?[1] There were earthquakes long ago, just as there are today.[2]

When all was still, Queen Nell could see that her strong palace had survived the quake. Then Nell walked outside the palace walls. Nell could see that her servants' homes had fallen during the quake.

Queen Nell said, "This is sad." Then Queen Nell asked, "Why did this happen?"

31

❶ **Inferring** (There was an earthquake.)

❷ **Teacher Think Aloud**

STORY COMPREHENSION

Use work pages from the workbook.

Monitoring Comprehension
Locating Information

Writing
Identifying—Who
Conventions—Period

Identifying—What

Writing
Describing
Conventions—Period

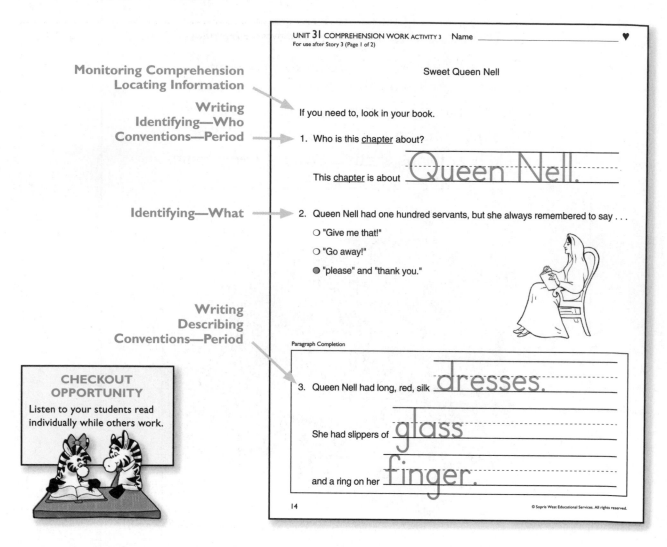

> UNIT **31** COMPREHENSION WORK ACTIVITY 3   Name _____ ♥
> For use after Story 3 (Page 1 of 2)
>
> Sweet Queen Nell
>
> If you need to, look in your book.
>
> 1. Who is this <u>chapter</u> about?
>
>   This <u>chapter</u> is about ___Queen Nell.___
>
> 2. Queen Nell had one hundred servants, but she always remembered to say . . .
>
>   ○ "Give me that!"
>
>   ○ "Go away!"
>
>   ● "please" and "thank you."
>
> Paragraph Completion
>
> 3. Queen Nell had long, red, silk ___dresses.___
>
>   She had slippers of ___glass___
>
>   and a ring on her ___finger.___
>
> 14   © Sopris West Educational Services. All rights reserved.

CHECKOUT OPPORTUNITY

Listen to your students read individually while others work.

PROCEDURES

For each step, demonstrate and guide practice as needed.

1. Sentence Completion—Basic Instructions (Items 1, 3, 4)

Have students read, complete each sentence, and end each sentence with a period.

2. Multiple Choice—Basic Instructions (Item 2)

Have students fill in the bubble for the correct answer. Periodically, think aloud with students. Discuss the multiple choice options. As appropriate, ask questions like: "Does the first answer make sense?" "Is that what the book said?" "Is the answer completely correct?"

3. Sentence Illustration—Specific Instructions (Item 5)

Have students read the sentence and then have them complete the illustration.

Writing Identifying—What Conventions—Period →

4. What did Queen Nell do all day?   (Accept answers in any order.)

• Queen Nell spent her days resting.

• She spent her days visiting.

• She spent her days reading.

• She spent her days singing.

Illustrating—Who, Action →

Sentence Illustration

5. Then one day, the earth began to quiver. Things began to tumble from the walls. Queen Nell hid under the big, strong bed.

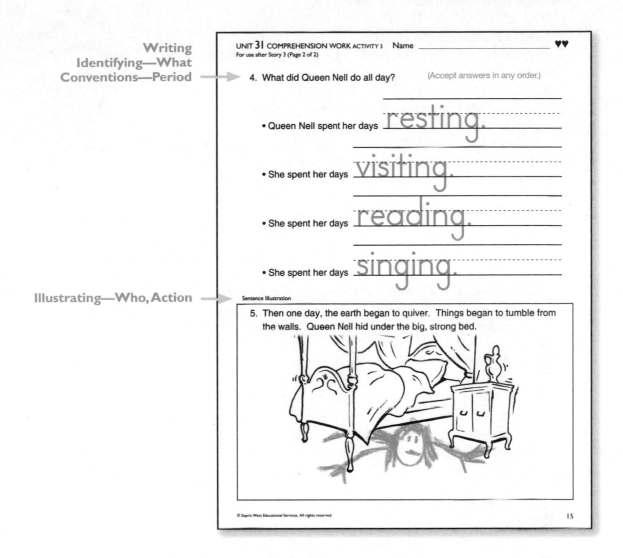

15

SOLO STORY READING INSTRUCTIONS
Students read from their own storybooks.

COMPREHENSION BUILDING:
DISCUSSION QUESTIONS AND TEACHER THINK ALOUDS
- Ask questions and discuss text on the *second* reading when indicated in the storybook in light gray text.
- Encourage students to answer questions with complete sentences when appropriate.
- If students have difficulty with a comprehension question, think aloud with them or reread the portion of the story that answers the question. Then, ask the question again.

PROCEDURES

1. First Reading
- Have students individually whisper read the story, using their fingers to track text.
- After students complete the first reading and before the second reading, have students practice a paragraph. First demonstrate expressive reading for students, then give individual turns. Acknowledge student efforts.

2. Second Reading
- Mix group and individual turns, independent of your voice. Have students work toward an accuracy goal of 0–2 errors. Quietly keep track of errors made by all students in each group.
- After reading the story, practice any difficult words.
- If the group has not reached the accuracy goal, have the group reread the story, mixing group and individual turns.

3. Repeated Readings
a. Timed Readings

- Once the accuracy goal has been achieved, have individual students read the page while the other children track the text with their fingers and whisper read. Time individuals for 30 seconds and encourage each student to work for a personal best.
- Count the number of words read correctly in 30 seconds (words read minus errors). Multiply by two to determine words correct per minute. Record student scores.

b. Partner Reading

During students' daily independent work, have them do Partner Reading.

c. Homework 2

Have students read the story at home. (A reprint of this story is available on a blackline master in *Read Well* Homework.)

STORY 4, SOLO

CHAPTER 2

Queen Nell Helps

What happened in the last chapter?[1]

All was not well in Queen Nell's kingdom. A big earthquake had left things a mess. The people were sad.

Queen Nell said, "This is bad. Please, let me help you." Then quick as a wink, Queen Nell began helping her people clean up.

The Queen and the people worked hard. Day after day, they worked together.

What did Queen Nell do?[2] How do you think that made the people feel?[3]

32

FOCUS ON EXPRESSION

After students complete the first reading and before the second reading, have them practice two or three sentences at a time. Demonstrate expressive reading, then give individual turns.

❶ **Summarizing** (There was a big earthquake in Queen Nell's kingdom. The servants' homes were ruined.)

❷ **Identifying—Action** (Queen Nell helped her people clean up.)

❸ **Inferring**

One day, a little kid said to Nell, "Queen Nell, you are a great worker! I want you to be my friend."

Nell grinned and said, "You are my friend too. We are a team."

Why did the child want Queen Nell to be her friend?[1]

Queen Nell said to her people, "We can build stronger buildings. We will build where the land is hard. We can work together!" The people nodded. They even sang as they worked.

33

❶ Inferring

36

STORY COMPREHENSION
Use work pages from the workbook.

Monitoring Comprehension
Locating Information

Writing, Identifying—Problem
Conventions—Period

Identifying—Action

Identifying—What

Identifying—What

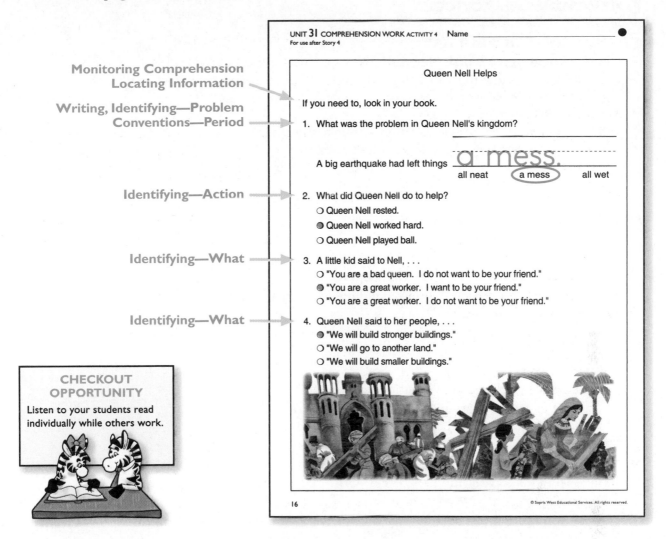

UNIT 31 COMPREHENSION WORK ACTIVITY 4   Name _____
For use after Story 4

Queen Nell Helps

If you need to, look in your book.

1. What was the problem in Queen Nell's kingdom?

   _____

   A big earthquake had left things _a mess._

   all neat   (a mess)   all wet

2. What did Queen Nell do to help?
   ○ Queen Nell rested.
   ● Queen Nell worked hard.
   ○ Queen Nell played ball.

3. A little kid said to Nell, . . .
   ○ "You are a bad queen. I do not want to be your friend."
   ● "You are a great worker. I want to be your friend."
   ○ "You are a great worker. I do not want to be your friend."

4. Queen Nell said to her people, . . .
   ● "We will build stronger buildings."
   ○ "We will go to another land."
   ○ "We will build smaller buildings."

16

© Sopris West Educational Services. All rights reserved.

CHECKOUT OPPORTUNITY
Listen to your students read individually while others work.

PROCEDURES
For each step, demonstrate and guide practice as needed.

1. **Multiple Choice, Sentence Completion—Basic Instructions** (Item 1)
   - Have students select and circle the word or words that correctly complete the sentence.
   - Have them write the answer in the blank and place a period at the end as appropriate.

2. **Multiple Choice—Basic Instructions** (Items 2, 3, 4)
   Have students fill in the bubble for the correct answer.

1 SOUND REVIEW

2 NEW SOUND PRACTICE

◆◆ **3** FOCUS ON VOCABULARY
Review vocabulary word: "legend"
Have students review the word "legend" and use it in a sentence. Say something like:
In the past, people would tell stories to explain the things they saw.
These stories are called *legends*.
What kind of story did people tell to explain things they saw? (Legends)
A story that explains why we have volcanoes is called a . . . (legend).
The "Legend of Pele" is a made-up story that explains why we have . . . (volcanoes).
A story that explains why we have earthquakes is called a . . . (legend).

4 SOUNDING OUT SMOOTHLY
Provide repeated practice. Mix group and individual turns, independent of your voice.

◆◆ **5** ACCURACY AND FLUENCY BUILDING
• Repeat practice on each column, building accuracy first and then fluency.
★ **New word pattern: /-old/**
• For the Circle Column, introduce the new word pattern /-old/. Say something like:
O-l-d spells "old."
Read the word. (old)
The next words rhyme with "old."
Read the underlined part and then the whole word. (old, hold, old, told)

6 TRICKY WORDS
★ **New Tricky Words: "cover" and "words"**
• Have students look at the new Tricky Word "cover." Say something like:
Try reading the Tricky Word to yourselves.
When you figure it out, hold up your thumbs, but keep the word a secret. **Wait.**
Everyone read the word.
If students have trouble with "cover," tell them the word.
• Have students read "cover" five times, and use it in oral sentences.
• Have students look at the new Tricky Word "words." Say something like:
Read the underlined part to yourselves.
When I count to three, everyone read the word. 1, 2, 3.
• Have students read "words" five times and use it in oral sentences.
• Have students read the row. Repeat, mixing group and individual turns, independent of your voice. Use the words in sentences as needed.

7 DAILY STORY READING
Proceed to the Unit 31 Storybook. See Daily Lesson Planning for pacing suggestions.

8 COMPREHENSION AND SKILL WORK ACTIVITY 5 AND/OR ACTIVITY 6
See pages 44, 45, and/or 49.

◆◆ For ELLs and children with language delays, provide repeated and extended practice with the language patterns. See page 10 for tips.

UNIT 31 DECODING PRACTICE 3
(For use with Stories 5 and 6)

1. SOUND REVIEW Use Sound Cards for Units 1–31 or Sound Review on Decoding Practice 4.

2. NEW SOUND PRACTICE Have students read, trace, and say /qu/.

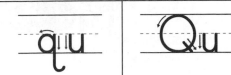

3. FOCUS ON VOCABULARY Review "legend." See the Teacher's Guide.

4. SOUNDING OUT SMOOTHLY Have students sound out each word in one smooth breath, then read the word.

▲   quick   glad   drop   quiver

★ 5. ACCURACY/FLUENCY BUILDING Have students read each word in the column. Next, have students practice the column.

♥	■	☆
under	listen	look
understand	listened	shook
✈	❀	●
after	grumble	★old
longer	tumble	h<u>old</u>
thinkers	rumble	t<u>old</u>

ACCURACY, THEN RATE
(Reminder)
Practice the words in each row or column until students can read the words with accuracy and confidence. Then work on gradually building speed. Say something like: Let's see if you can read the Heart and Airplane Columns about this fast . . .

★ 6. TRICKY WORDS See Teacher's Guide for how to introduce "cover" and "words." Next, have students silently figure out each word and read it aloud.

✎ They   ★cover   Listen   friends   ★<u>words</u>

◆◆ **SENTENCE SUGGESTIONS**

● old – If you live to be 100, you are . . . old.

⬟ hold – Show me how to hold [onto the table].

✎ cover – Cover your eyes.

7. DAILY STORY READING

7

Sentence Suggestions: Use the appropriate suggested sentence *after* decoding each individual word.

DUET STORY READING INSTRUCTIONS

Students read from their own storybooks.

The teacher reads the small text and students read the large text.

PACING

- 3- to 4-Day Plans: Have students do the first reading
  of Duet Story 5.

  Then proceed to repeated readings of Solo Story 6.

- 6- to 10-Day Plans: Have students do the first *and*
  second readings.

COMPREHENSION BUILDING:
DISCUSSION QUESTIONS AND TEACHER THINK ALOUDS

- Ask questions and discuss text on the first reading when indicated in
  the storybook in light gray text.
- Encourage students to answer questions with complete sentences
  when appropriate.
- If students have difficulty with a comprehension question, think aloud
  with them or reread the portion of the story that answers the question.
  Then, ask the question again.

PROCEDURES

1. Summarizing

Have students review who and what the story is about. Say something like:

This is Chapter 3 of "The Legend of Queen Nell." Who is the main character?

(Queen Nell is the main character.)

What happened in Queen Nell's kingdom?

(There was a big earthquake. It left things a mess.)

What did Queen Nell do to help her people?

(She helped clean up. She helped them build new homes.)

2. First Reading

Mix group and individual turns on student-read sentences. On individual
turns, gently correct any error, and then have the student reread the text.

3. Second Reading

Repeat the reading only as needed for comprehension.

CHAPTER 3

The Thinkers Tell a Legend

What is a legend?[1] What do you think will happen in this chapter?[2]

The people were happy with their new homes. Still, they worried and wanted to know why the earth had rumbled and roared.

Queen Nell went to the thinkers of her land. She said, "We do not understand why the earth was so mad. Why did the earth grumble and quiver? Please tell us why the earth shook so hard."

What did Queen Nell want to understand?[3]

One thinker said, "The earth is not mad."

The thinkers were as puzzled as Queen Nell. They did not know what made the earth shake, but they also knew that the people would be sad until they understood why the earth had rumbled and rolled. So, the second thinker said, "Well, the earth is very heavy—too heavy for the four elephants."

Queen Nell asked, "What elephants?"

Then the second thinker said, "Oh, the elephants that hold up the earth."

Then the third thinker said, "Yes, and the four elephants are standing on the back of a turtle."

And the fourth thinker added, "It is very hard for that turtle to balance on the cobra! Imagine that!"

Queen Nell closed her eyes and tried to imagine the earth sitting on four elephants that stood on top of the turtle that balanced on top of a cobra.

34

FOCUS ON VOCABULARY

After reading the title of the chapter, say something like: The thinkers are going to tell a legend. A legend is a story that . . . explains why something happens. What do you think the thinkers are going to explain?

VISUALIZING

After completing the page, say something like: The thinkers are using their imaginations and coming up with quite a story about the earthquake.

I'm going to read to the bottom of page 34 again.

Close your eyes and try to picture what the thinkers are telling Queen Nell.

Did you imagine four elephants holding up the earth?

What were the elephants standing on top of?

What was the turtle balancing on?

Before you open your eyes, imagine the elephants moving. What would happen?

❶ **Defining Vocabulary—Legend** (Legends are stories people made up to explain the things they saw.)

❷ **Predicting**

❸ **Explaining** (Queen Nell wanted to understand why the earth shook so hard.)

What are the thinkers trying to explain? **I**

35

❶ **Inferring** (The thinkers are trying to explain why there was an earthquake.)

Queen Nell listened to the thinkers. Then she said, "My, the animals must be strong. It must be hard to stand still year after year."

The thinkers nodded and were glad.

Then Queen Nell said, "Please tell the people why the earth shook. Then tell them what to do."

The thinkers said, "We will do as you wish. We will tell the people to drop, cover, and hold on."

Queen Nell said, "Thank you."

Why did Queen Nell thank the thinkers? **1**The thinkers didn't know why the earth shook, so they made up a story. The thinkers did know what the people should do if there was an earthquake. What did the thinkers say they should do?**2**

36

❶ **Inferring** (Queen Nell thanked the thinkers because they explained why there was an earthquake, and because they will tell the people what to do.)

❷ **Identifying—What** (They should drop, cover, and hold on.)

43

STORY MAP

Use work pages from the workbook.

Writing, Summarizing, Sequencing
Conventions—Period

Monitoring Comprehension
Locating Information

Explaining—Beginning
Identifying—Who

Describing

Explaining—Middle
Identifying—Action

Identifying—Problem

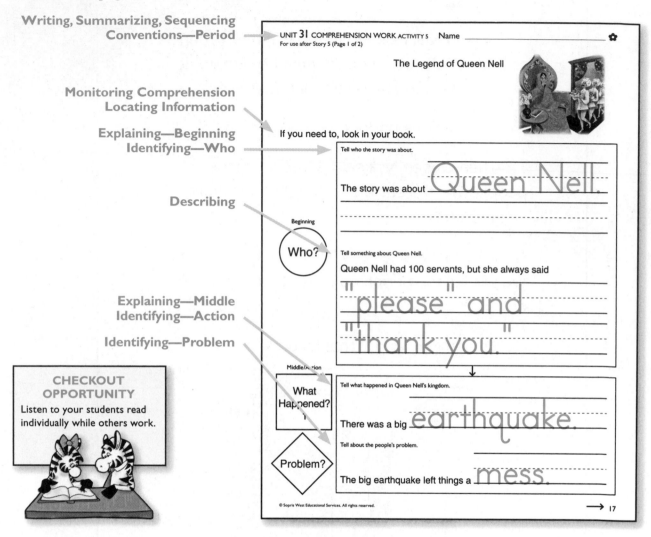

UNIT **31** COMPREHENSION WORK ACTIVITY 5   Name _____
For use after Story 5 (Page 1 of 2)

The Legend of Queen Nell

If you need to, look in your book.

Tell who the story was about.

The story was about Queen Nell.

Beginning
Who?

Tell something about Queen Nell.

Queen Nell had 100 servants, but she always said

"please" and "thank you."

Middle/Action
What Happened?

Tell what happened in Queen Nell's kingdom.

There was a big earthquake.

Problem?

Tell about the people's problem.

The big earthquake left things a mess.

→ 17

CHECKOUT OPPORTUNITY

Listen to your students read individually while others work.

PROCEDURES

For each step, demonstrate and guide practice as needed.

Story Map—Basic Instructions

- Using a blank or overhead copy of the story map, help students identify the basic story elements—who the story is about, what happened in the story, what the problem was, and what happened at the end.
- Have students fill in the blanks to create a story map of "The Legend of Queen Nell."
- Remind students that a story map helps them retell or summarize the important parts of a story.

Note: You may wish to remind students that a sentence ends with a period.

Explaining

Explaining—End

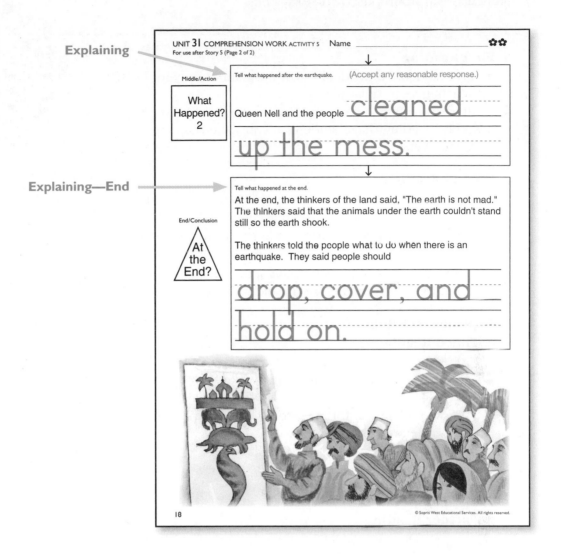

UNIT **31** COMPREHENSION WORK ACTIVITY 5   Name _____   ✿✿
For use after Story 5 (Page 2 of 2)

Middle/Action

What
Happened?
2

Tell what happened after the earthquake.   (Accept any reasonable response.)

Queen Nell and the people __cleaned__
__up the mess.__

End/Conclusion

At
the
End?

Tell what happened at the end.

At the end, the thinkers of the land said, "The earth is not mad."
The thinkers said that the animals under the earth couldn't stand
still so the earth shook.

The thinkers told the people what to do when there is an
earthquake. They said people should

__drop, cover, and__
__hold on.__

18

SOLO STORY READING INSTRUCTIONS
Students read from their own storybooks.

PROCEDURES

1. First Reading
- Have students individually whisper read the poem, using their fingers to track text.

 • After students complete the first reading and before the second reading, have students identify the rhyming words in each verse.

2. Second Reading
- Mix group and individual turns, independent of your voice. Have students work toward an accuracy goal of 0–2 errors. Quietly keep track of errors made by all students in each group.
- After reading the story, practice any difficult words.
- If the group has not reached the accuracy goal, have the group reread the story, mixing group and individual turns.

3. Repeated Readings
a. Timed Readings

 • Once the accuracy goal has been achieved, have individual students read the page while the other children track the text with their fingers and whisper read. Time individuals for 30 seconds and encourage each student to work for a personal best.
- Count the number of words read correctly in 30 seconds (words read minus errors). Multiply by two to determine words correct per minute. Record student scores.

b. Partner Reading

 During students' daily independent work, have them do Partner Reading.

c. Homework 3

 Have students read the story at home. (A reprint of this story is available on a blackline master in *Read Well* Homework.)

Drop, Cover, and Hold

What is the title of this poem? ¹

Listen, my friends,
And you will hear
Of the earthquake's rumble
And the people's fear.

When the earth was mad,
It shook and shook.
The people could hear.
The people could look.

Things began to fall.
Things began to shatter.
Things began to tumble.
Things began to clatter.

"Help! Help!
We are so mad!
Help! Help!
We are so sad!"

"We need a plan.
The plan we pick
Should be fast
And should be quick."

37

❶ **Identifying—Title** (The title of the poem is "Drop, Cover, and Hold.")

STORY 6, SOLO

The people did ask
And they were told,
Three little words,
Drop, cover, hold.

The people nodded
And were glad.
The people were
No longer sad.

The people did ask
And they were told,
Three little words,
Drop, cover, hold.

FOCUS ON EXPRESSION

After the first reading, have students practice one or two verses at a time. Demonstrate how to read the poem within the children's reading rate, but with the rhythm and cadence of a poem. Avoid an overly sing-songy voice.

38

RHYMING PATTERNS

Use work pages from the workbook.

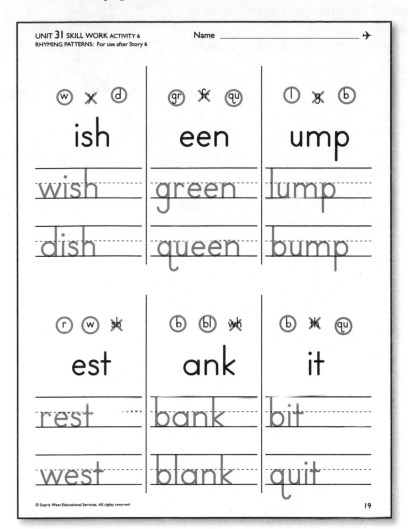

PROCEDURES

Demonstrate and guide practice as needed.

Rhyming Patterns—Basic Instructions

For each box, have students:

• Read the rhyming pattern.
• Circle the two sounds above the rhyming pattern that go with it to make real words.
• Cross out the sound that does not make a real word with the rhyming pattern.
• Write the two rhyming words on the lines provided.

Note: For students who struggle or who lack the English language base to know which are real words, you may wish to identify the two sounds they should circle in each box. Students can then write the pattern words on their own.

Note: There are multiple uses for Decoding Practice 4.

- Have students practice a few rows and/or columns each day.
- Use the whole page at the end of the unit for fluency building and/or to informally assess skills.
- Have students complete the page as a partner review or take it home to practice.
- Build spelling dictation lessons using the sounds and words on this page.

❶ SOUND REVIEW

❷ ACCURACY AND FLUENCY BUILDING

In the Two-Flower Column, have students practice the difficult /qu/ sound by identifying the underlined part first, then reading the whole word. If students need more help on /qu/, demonstrate how to sound the words out smoothly. Emphasize how to blend smoothly from /qu/ to the vowel.

❸ TRICKY WORDS

❹ MULTISYLLABIC CHALLENGE WORDS

❺ DAILY STORY READING

See Daily Lesson Planning for story suggestions.

FLUENCY, FLUENCY, FLUENCY!
Accurate, Smooth, and Confident Reading

- Have students practice the Tricky Words in these decoding pages until they can read all the words automatically and with no errors.
- Put the Solo Stories from previous units into a binder. Have students practice reading the stories in partners.
- Have students read a Solo Story into a tape recorder, listen to themselves, and then read the story again—working on making their reading more fluent.

UNIT 31 DECODING PRACTICE 4
(See Daily Lesson Planning for story suggestions.)

1. SOUND REVIEW Set pace. Have students read the sounds in each row.

▲	qu	m	ea	y	a	W	o	7
■	f	er	c	Qu	b	i	v	14
♥	e	j	u	sh	P	ar	g	21

2. ACCURACY/FLUENCY BUILDING For each column, have students say any underlined part, then read each word. Next, have students read the column.

✈	✈✈	✈✈✈	❀	❀❀
pick	fall	vet	<u>a</u>way	qu<u>ack</u>
stick	ball	pet	<u>a</u>go	qu<u>ick</u>
brick	call	met	<u>a</u>cross	qu<u>ilt</u>
trick	tall	wet	<u>a</u>gree	qu<u>it</u>
click	hall	get	<u>a</u>bout	qu<u>een</u>

3. TRICKY WORDS Have students silently figure out each word and then read it aloud.

☆☆	what	you	there	of	should
☆☆	They	has	from	two	isn't
☆☆	please	earth	people	were	

4. MULTISYLLABIC CHALLENGE WORDS Have students say each word part, then read the whole word.

ban•quets = banquets	squig•gle = squiggle
quin•tu•plets = quintuplets	e•quip•ment = equipment

5. DAILY STORY READING

8

BLACKOUT BINGO (Reminder)
Periodically, use the Decoding Practice pages to play a modified Blackout Bingo. Give each student an opportunity to read a word of his or her choice. Then have students find and cover the word on their Decoding Practice with a game marker.

End of the Unit

In this section, you will find:

Making Decisions

As you near the end of the unit, you will need to make decisions. Should you administer the Oral Reading Fluency Assessment or should you teach Extra Practice lessons?

Unit 31 Oral Reading Fluency Assessment

The Unit 31 Oral Reading Fluency Assessment is located on page 54 and can also be found in the *Assessment Manual*.

Certificate of Achievement

Celebrate your children's accomplishments.

Extra Practice

Lessons and blackline masters for added decoding practice and independent work are provided for students who need extended practice opportunities.

Making Decisions

ASSESSMENT READINESS

Assess when students are able to easily complete decoding tasks from the beginning of a lesson.

- If you aren't sure whether students are ready for the assessment, give the assessment. Do Extra Practice lessons if needed.
- If students are not ready for the assessment, proceed to Extra Practice lessons. Administer the assessment as soon as students are ready.

GENERAL ASSESSMENT GUIDELINES

- Assess all students.
- Assess each child individually.
- Score student responses on the Student Assessment Record, adhering to the scoring criteria in the *Assessment Manual*. Use a stopwatch to time how long it takes the student to read the oral fluency passage.
- Follow the general instructions at the bottom of each assessment. Record a Strong Pass, a Pass, a Weak Pass, or a No Pass.

ACCELERATION

- If students read with 100% accuracy and exceed the fluency goal, consider shortening units.
- If an individual student reads with greater fluency than others in his or her group, consider regrouping.

INTERVENTION OPTIONS—INDIVIDUALS
(WEAK PASS, NO PASS)

1. Add informal practice throughout the day.
2. Add practice with repeated readings on Solo Stories.
3. Find ways to provide a double dose of *Read Well* instruction.
   - Have the student work in his or her group *and* a lower group.
   - Have an instructional assistant, older student, or parent volunteer preview or review lessons.
   - Have an instructional assistant provide instruction with Extra Practice lessons.
4. Consider placement in a lower group. If one child's fluency scores are significantly lower than the other children in the group, success will be impossible without additional and intensive practice.

INTERVENTION OPTIONS—GROUP (WEAK PASS, NO PASS)

1. Extend the unit with Extra Practice lessons.
2. Consider a Jell Well Review before moving forward. (See the *Assessment Manual*.)

CERTIFICATE OF ACHIEVEMENT

When students pass the assessment, celebrate with the Certificate of Achievement. Then, set a personal goal. (See *Getting Started*.)

> ### ASSESSING UNPRACTICED READING
>
> Do not have children practice the assessments. The goal of reading instruction is to provide children with the skills to read independently. Repeated readings are an excellent tool for building fluency; however, the end-of-the-unit assessment is designed to assess how well students transfer their skills to unrehearsed passages.

TRICKY WORD WARM-UP

from	animals	father	of	even

ORAL READING FLUENCY PASSAGE

My Brother

☆ My brother bugs me. One day he said, "You have   10
hundreds of ants in your room."   16

I said, "Stop. Do not play tricks. I have never had ants   28
in my room."   31

He said, "You better be quick. Ants are under your bed.   42
Soon they will be in your bed."   49

I said, "Bill, quit that. You always try to trick me."   60

Bill said, "You better go look."   66

ORAL READING FLUENCY	Start timing at the ☆ Mark errors. Make a single slash in the text (/) at 60 seconds. Have student complete passage. If the student completes the passage in less than 60 seconds, have the student go back to the ☆ and continue reading. Make a double slash (//) in the text at 60 seconds.
WCPM	Determine words correct per minute by subtracting errors from words read in 60 seconds.
STRONG PASS	The student scores no more than 2 errors on the first pass through the passage and reads a minimum of 80 or more words correct per minute. Proceed to Unit 32.
PASS	The student scores no more than 2 errors on the first pass through the passage and reads 66 to 79 words correct per minute. Proceed to Unit 32.
WEAK PASS	The student scores no more than 2 errors on the first pass through the passage and reads 53 to 65 words correct per minute. Proceed to Unit 32 with added fluency practice, or provide Extra Practice lessons in Unit 31, and/or provide a Jell-Well Review.
NO PASS	The student scores 3 or more errors on the first pass through the passage and/or reads 52 or fewer words correct per minute. Provide Extra Practice lessons and retest, and/or provide a Jell-Well Review.

Certificate of Achievement

This certifies that

_____,

on this _____ day of _____, _____,

has successfully completed

Read Well Unit 31

Sounds Mastered: s, e, ee, m, a, d, th, n, t, w, i, Th, h, c, r, ea, sh, k, -ck, oo, ar, wh, ě, -y (as in "fly"), l, o, b, all, g, f, u, -er, oo (as in "book"), y, a (schwa), p, ay, v, qu

Known Words: By Unit 30, you had learned and practiced 853 words.

New Words Mastered in Unit 31: build, buildings, cover, earthquake, earthquakes, earthquake's, listened, people's, please, servants, very, worker, agree, always, apartment, bam, banquets, brick, bump, castle, clatter, click, clump, crashing, days, dresses, equipment, fear, finger, fingers, glass, hall, hearing, helping, helps, hold, hop, hopping, hugs, kingdom, left, longer, lump, Nell, Nell's, old, quack, queen, quick, quilt, quintuplets, quit, quiver, reading, remembered, shatter, shook, silk, silver, singing, slipper, slippers, spent, squiggle, stronger, stump, sudden, thinker, thinkers, told, tumble, vet, visiting, walls, whatever, within, yelled, yelling

You can now read 931 words—plus many other words made up of the sounds and patterns you've learned.

Note: Personal and Team Goal Setting forms can be copied from Units 16 and 17, or from *Getting Started.*

❶ SOUNDS

Have students say each sound.

❷ WORD DICTATION

try, bed, He, room

The first word is "try." We're going to count the sounds in "try."
Tell me the first sound. **Hold up one finger.** (/t/)
Repeat with /rrr/ and /-yyy/.
How many sounds are in "try"? (Three)

Tell me the first sound. (/t/) Write it.
Repeat with /rrr/ and /-yyy/.
Do Smooth Blending. (/trrryyy/) Read the word. (try)

Repeat with "bed," "He," and "room."

CAUTION

Your children may not need Extra Practice. If in doubt, assess students and include Extra Practice only if needed.

DICTATION

• Demonstrate and guide practice as needed.

• Have students check and correct.

❸ SENTENCE COMPLETION

I have ants *in my bed*.

• Have students read the beginning of the sentence with you.
• Dictate each of the last three words "in my bed." Tell students to leave a finger space between each word. Remind students to end the sentence with a period.
• Have students trace the dotted words.
• Have students read the sentence.

❹ ACCURACY AND FLUENCY BUILDING

Repeat practice on each column, building accuracy first and then fluency.

❺ TRICKY WORDS

Repeat practice, mixing group and individual turns, independent of your voice.

❻ DAILY STORY READING

1. First Reading

Have students choral read the Fluency Passage.

2. Second Reading

• Provide individual turns on sentences. Quietly keep track of errors.
• After reading, practice any difficult words.

3. Repeated Readings
   a. Timed Readings

• Have individual students read the passage while other students track the text with their fingers and whisper read. Time individuals for 30 seconds. Encourage students to work for a personal best.
• For each student, count the number of words read correctly in 30 seconds (words read minus errors). Multiply by two to determine words correct per minute. Record students' scores.

   b. Partner Reading—Checkout Opportunity

While students are partner reading, listen to individuals read the passage.

1. SOUNDS Have students say each sound.

Qu	er	v	P	o	oo	sh	Y
ay	ar	qu	h	W	p	ee	e

2. WORD DICTATION Have students count the sounds in each word, identify and write each sound, and then read the word: "try," "bed," "He," and "room."

1 _____ 2 _____ 3 _____ 4 _____

3. SENTENCE COMPLETION Have students read the beginning of the sentence. Dictate "in my bed." Have students trace the words and complete the sentence with a period.

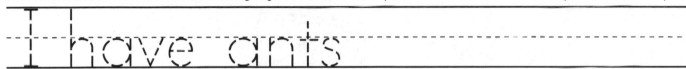

I have ants

4. ACCURACY/FLUENCY BUILDING In each column, have students say any underlined part, then read each word. Next, have students read the column.

♥	♥♥	♥♥♥
<u>qu</u>ick	day	<u>a</u>nts
<u>qu</u>ack	play	<u>s</u>oon
<u>qu</u>it	way	tr<u>i</u>ck
<u>qu</u>een	<u>ways</u>	b<u>u</u>gs
<u>qu</u>ilt	al<u>ways</u>	st<u>o</u>p

5. TRICKY WORDS For each word, have students silently figure out the word, then read it aloud.

brother	are	from	even	your

6. DAILY STORY READING

Name_____

FLUENCY PASSAGE

A Quick Quake

Bill and I were in an earthquake the other day.   10
There was a quiver, and the earth shook. We got   20
under my bed. My brother said, "I want this to stop."   31

When things quit crashing, my brother said,   38
"That was a big earthquake!"   43

I said, "I'm glad it was quick."   50

My personal best is ____ words correct per minute.
My goal is to read with 0–2 errors. This is what I did:

Have students read the sentences. Time individual students for 30 seconds; mark errors. To determine words correct per minute (wcpm), count words read in 30 seconds, subtract errors, multiply times two, and record on the chart. If the student completes the passage in less than 30 seconds, have him or her return to the top and continue reading. (Repeated readings may be completed with older blackmen, assistants, or parents.)

Reading	1st	2nd	3rd	4th
Errors				
Words/ 30 seconds				
wcpm				

58

Take-Home Game

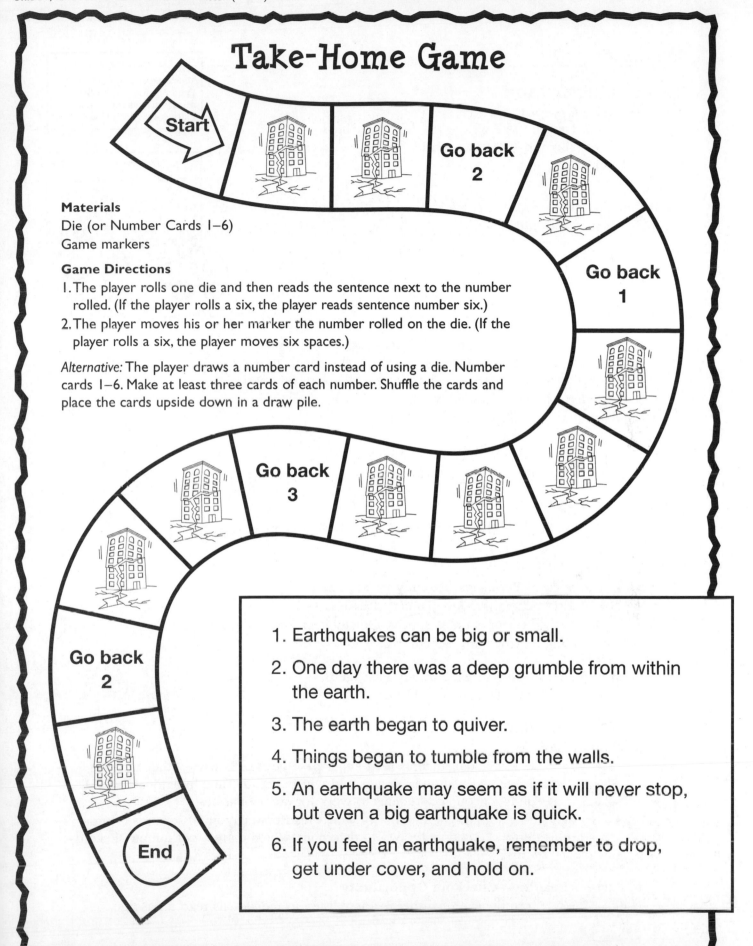

Start

Go back 2

Go back 1

Go back 3

Go back 2

End

Materials

Die (or Number Cards 1–6)
Game markers

Game Directions

1. The player rolls one die and then reads the sentence next to the number rolled. (If the player rolls a six, the player reads sentence number six.)
2. The player moves his or her marker the number rolled on the die. (If the player rolls a six, the player moves six spaces.)

Alternative: The player draws a number card instead of using a die. Number cards 1–6. Make at least three cards of each number. Shuffle the cards and place the cards upside down in a draw pile.

1. Earthquakes can be big or small.

2. One day there was a deep grumble from within the earth.

3. The earth began to quiver.

4. Things began to tumble from the walls.

5. An earthquake may seem as if it will never stop, but even a big earthquake is quick.

6. If you feel an earthquake, remember to drop, get under cover, and hold on.

1 SOUNDS

2 WORD DICTATION

had, that, stop, quit

The first word is "had." We're going to count the sounds in "had."

Tell me the first sound. **Hold up one finger.** (/h/)

Repeat with /aaa/ and /d/.

How many sounds are in "had"? (Three)

Tell me the first sound. (/h/) Write it.

Repeat with /aaa/ and /d/.

Do Smooth Blending. (/haaad/) Read the word. (had)

Repeat with "that," "stop," and "quit."

3 SENTENCE COMPLETION

Look *at me.*

- Have students read the beginning of the sentence with you.
- Dictate each of the last two words "at me." Tell students to leave a finger space between each word. Remind students to end the sentence with a period.
- Have students trace the dotted word.
- Have students read the sentence.

4 ACCURACY AND FLUENCY BUILDING

Repeat practice on each column, building accuracy first and then fluency.

5 TRICKY WORDS

Repeat practice, mixing group and individual turns, independent of your voice.

6 DAILY STORY READING

1. First and Second Readings, Fluency Passage A
- Have students choral read the Fluency Passage.
- Provide individual turns on sentences. Quietly keep track of errors.
- After reading, practice any difficult words.

2. First and Second Readings, Fluency Passage B
Repeat step one with Fluency Passage B.

3. Repeated Readings
a. Timed Readings

- Have individual students read either passage A or B while other students track the text with their fingers and whisper read. Time individuals for 30 seconds. Encourage students to work for a personal best.
- For each student, count the number of words read correctly in 30 seconds (words read minus errors). Multiply by two to determine words correct per minute. Record students' scores.

b. Partner Reading—Checkout Opportunity

While students are partner reading, listen to individuals read a passage.

CAUTION

Your children may not need Extra Practice. If in doubt, assess students and include Extra Practice only if needed.

HAVE STUDENTS CHECK AND CORRECT.

Name_____

1. SOUNDS Have students say each sound.

v	ea	m	a	qu	o	V	er
Qu	i	y	e	b	u	ay	g

2. WORD DICTATION Have students count the sounds in each word, identify and write each sound, and then read the word: "had," "that," "stop," and "quit."

1 _____   2 _____   3 _____   4 _____

3. SENTENCE COMPLETION Have students read the beginning of the sentence. Dictate "at me." Have students trace the words and complete the sentence with a period.

Look

4. ACCURACY/FLUENCY BUILDING In each column, have students say any underlined part, then read each word. Next, have students read the column.

♥	♥♥	♥♥♥
<u>qu</u>een	h<u>a</u>ve	father
<u>qu</u>it	r<u>oo</u>m	brother
<u>qu</u>ilt	w<u>ill</u>	better
<u>qu</u>ick	b<u>e</u>d	never
<u>qu</u>ack	h<u>u</u>ndreds	under

5. TRICKY WORDS For each word, have students silently figure out the word, then read it aloud.

because	father	of	You	animals

6. DAILY STORY READING

Name_____

FLUENCY PASSAGE A

The Big Quake

My father said, "That was an earthquake. It was   9
fast, but it was big."   14
My sister said, "Why did we have an   22
earthquake?"   23
My father said, "Let's read about earthquakes."   30

FLUENCY PASSAGE B

What to Do

My mother said, "If you hear a rumble, drop,   9
cover, and hold on."   13
My father said, "Remember, if there is an   21
earthquake, do not play. Get under the bed and   30
hold on."   32

My personal best is _____ words correct per minute.

My goal is to read with 0–2 errors. This is what I did:

Have students read the sentences. Time individual students for 30 seconds on one passage; mark errors. To determine words correct per minute (wcpm), count words read in 30 seconds, subtract errors, multiply times two, and record on the chart. If the student completes the passage in less than 30 seconds, have him or her return to the top and continue reading. (Repeated readings may be completed with older students, assistants, or parents.)

Reading	1st	2nd	3rd	4th
Errors				
Words/ 30 seconds				
wcpm				

❶ STORYBOOK DECODING REVIEW

For each row, mix group and individual turns, independent of your voice.

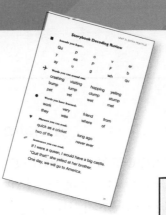

❷ WORD DICTATION

Have students count the sounds in each word with their fingers, identify and write each sound, and then read the word. Use the words in sentences as needed.

soon, day, ants, had

The first word is "soon." We're going to count the sounds in "soon." Tell me the first sound. **Hold up one finger.** (/sss/)

Repeat with /oooo/ and /nnn/.
How many sounds are in "soon"? (Three)

Tell me the first sound. (/sss/) Write it.

Repeat with /oooo/ and /nnn/.
Do Smooth Blending. (/sssoooonnn/) Read the word. (soon)

Repeat with "day," "ants," and "had."

CAUTION

Your children may not need Extra Practice. If in doubt, assess students and include Extra Practice only if needed.

HAVE STUDENTS CHECK AND CORRECT.

❸ DAILY STORY READING

1. First Reading

Have students choral read the Fluency Passage.

2. Second Reading

- Provide individual turns on sentences. Quietly keep track of errors made by all students in the group.
- After reading, practice any difficult words.

3. Repeated Readings
a. Timed Readings

- Have individual students read the passage while other students track the text with their fingers and whisper read. Time individuals for 60 seconds. Encourage students to work for a personal best.
- For each student, count the number of words read correctly in 60 seconds (words read minus errors). Determine words correct per minute. Record students' scores.

b. Partner Reading—Checkout Opportunity

While students are partner reading, listen to individuals read the passage. Work on accuracy or fluency as needed.

Name_____

FLUENCY PASSAGE

What a Mess!

Did you feel that earthquake? We could feel the	9
earth quiver and we could hear the glass shatter as	19
things began to fall. It was a big earthquake but it was	31
quick. We hid until things quit crashing. After the	40
earthquake, the apartment was one big mess. We	48
worked hard to clean it up.	54

My personal best is _____ words correct per minute.
My goal is to read with 0–2 errors. This is what I did:

Have students read the sentences. Time individual students for 30 seconds; mark errors. To determine words correct per minute (wcpm), count words read in 30 seconds, subtract errors, multiply times two, and record on the chart. If the student completes the passage in less than 30 seconds, have him or her return to the top and continue reading. (Repeated readings may be completed with older students, assistants, or parents.)

Reading	1st	2nd	3rd	4th
Errors				
Words/ 30 seconds				
wcpm				

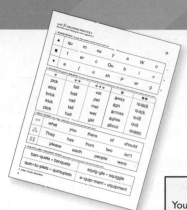

1 **DECODING PRACTICE 4 REVIEW**

For each row, mix group and individual turns, independent of your voice.

2 **WORD DICTATION**

Have students count the sounds in each word with their fingers, identify and write each sound, and then read the word. Use the words in sentences as needed.

that, try, bugs, he

The first word is "that." We're going to count the sounds in "that."
Tell me the first sound. **Hold up one finger.** (/ththth/)
Repeat with /aaa/ and /t/.
How many sounds are in "that"? (Three)

Tell me the first sound. (/ththth/) Write it.
Repeat with /aaa/ and /t/.
Do Smooth Blending. (/ththaaat/) Read the word. (that)
Repeat with "try," "bugs," and "he."

3 **DAILY STORY READING**

1. First Reading
Have students choral read the Fluency Passage.

2. Second Reading
- Provide individual turns on sentences. Quietly keep track of errors made by all students in the group.
- After reading, practice any difficult words.

3. Repeated Readings
a. Timed Readings

- Have individual students read the passage while other students track the text with their fingers and whisper read. Time individuals for 60 seconds. Encourage students to work for a personal best.
- For each student, count the number of words read correctly in 60 seconds (words read minus errors). Record students' scores.

b. Partner Reading—Checkout Opportunity

While students are partner reading, listen to individuals read the passage. Work on accuracy or fluency as needed.

CAUTION

Your children may not need Extra Practice. If in doubt, assess students and include Extra Practice only if needed.

HAVE STUDENTS CHECK AND CORRECT.

Name_____

FLUENCY PASSAGE

Jets in the Sky

A week ago I spotted some small dots in the sky.	11
There seemed to be just two or three. It was hard to	23
tell because they were so little.	29
I jumped up and said, "Look at the jets!"	38
"What did you say?" my sister asked.	45
I said, "There are jets in the sky. Come see."	55
My sister said, "I see the spots, but you have a	66
problem. The spots are not jets. They are eagles."	75

My personal best is _____ words correct per minute.

My goal is to read with 0–2 errors. This is what I did:

Have students read the sentences. Time individual students for 60 seconds; mark errors. To determine words correct per minute (wcpm), count words read in 60 seconds, subtract errors, and record on the chart. If the student completes the passage in less than 60 seconds, have him or her return to the top and continue reading. (Repeated readings may be completed with older students, assistants, or parents.)

Reading	1st	2nd	3rd	4th
Errors				
Words/ 60 seconds				
wcpm				